Winter Tennis

By the Same Author

TODD SWIFT

Winter Tennis

LIVRES **DC** BOOKS

Cover illustration by Josée Bisaillon. Author photograph by Derek Adams.
Book designed and typeset in Adobe Garamond Pro and Myriad MM by
Primeau & Barey, Montreal. Edited by Steve Luxton.

Copyright © Todd Swift, 2007.
Legal Deposit, *Bibliothèque et Archives nationales du Québec*
and the National Library of Canada, 1st trimester, 2007.

Library and Archives Canada Cataloguing in Publication
Swift, Todd, 1966-
Winter Tennis/Todd Swift.
Poems.
ISBN 978-1-897190-29-6 (pbk.)
ISBN 978-1-897190-30-2 (bound).
1. Title.
PS8587.W5W55 2007 C811'.54 C2007-901624-3

For our publishing activities, DC Books gratefully acknowledges the financial
support of the Canada Council for the Arts, of SODEC, and of the Government
of Canada through the Book Publishing Industry Development Program (BPIDP).

 Canada Council **Conseil des Arts** *Société de développement des entreprises culturelles*
for the Arts **du Canada**
Québec

Printed and bound in Canada by AGMV Marquis. Interior pages printed
on 100 per cent recycled and FSC certified Silva Enviro 110 white paper.
Distributed by Lit DistCo.

DC Books
PO Box 666, Station Saint-Laurent
Montreal, Quebec H4L 4V9
www.dcbooks.ca

This book is
for my father
Tom E. Swift

b. 1939–d. 2006

Contents

I.

*Lately the silence drives him
mutteringly mad, and the snow
blinds him.*

Robert Allen

Tomsk

*"... the Siberian Athens, known for its lacy
wooden buildings, furs, gold and universities."*
Local Tourist Guide

What are lacy buildings? Was there ever
a cold Socrates, a Parthenon gilded in ice?
What long poetry, what Pythagorean tears
scattered in these bitter white winds?
What polar bears bit at what rinds?
Did Plato and Aristotle, pulled by a team
of snow-caped malamutes, decamp in Tomsk
to envision gold-smeared Greece
reborn in a frozen swamp, newly lit
by Diogenes' lamp? Did they flame
the chill-gnawed Siberian landscape
with images of icons and geometry?

What exists love says should be:
a dolphin-grey, a book-kissed, city.

Auden in Snow

You come towards me no bigger than a thumb,
coated shabbily as Delmore Schwartz,
down some nameless New York street

from dive to blizzard, your face
that familiar map of crumpled age
as if manhandled by a foe of Thirties verse.

You go through the bright cold confetti
of the image, on straight into the lens,
both hands pocketed, secure in the stroll.

Gentlemen of Nerve

I have become my neighbour or the author or the man
I saw in the photo, when I was thirteen; I've slipped in
To his life, the one where you get to be the has-been

Movie writer; get to be the fellow who adores his wife;
The forty-year-old who walks slowly down boulevards
In springtime, thinking of nothing much, sidling along

With a mumble, instead of a song, in his punctured heart;
Now I know what they were doing when they were
Doing it; not exactly, for that was their lot, then; but well

Enough to hum the approximate ontology they unknit.
I have slipped in to the opening along their side,
Entered the weave of their nearby manhood, to coincide

With the shyness of a gentle soul who holds out
For some other day, some boon, a grand foretold
Coming in to confidence (and confidences); a Chump

At Oxford in a silk-lined coat who'd jump a fence
To avoid a bullying leaf or an unkind glance; a gentleman
Gentled by nothing so much as having sort of grown old

Without having ever advanced, in terms of career,
In terms of science, beyond the fields of expectant fear
That the sweet girl who holds him tight might evaporate

And all his books, thoughts and friends will disappear
Like stars, which look quite risky in the sky. So if
I am this guy, where is he now, past having had his own

Slippage moment, when he came into his three-piece Geist?
He might have driven far, stopped at the coast, for a well-
Earned cigar, maestro of leaning knowingly into a sea breeze;

For, the exact moment I turned forty and had insight into *him*
He was set free, to flow or saunter at unidentified ease, no
Longer a person observed or wondered at, but a ghostly skim

Of atoms, then other particles wafting to some inexact home,
As a genie exceeds the prison house of his wishes, to fly late
But gladly beyond the bottle's stoppered rim; so now I hesitate,

Poised, a diver on the doorframe of my impressionable
      bungalow,
My blissful villa, my flat, my porch, my mansion, my estate—
Until some kid spies me out as curious, unimaginably aged, so

When their grey stubble hits the marker they'll zap to my face,
Slip in to my statehood, reassemble a mixed-blessings-self
      or two,
While, sweet as rain after drought, I dance out and over as I go.

Emperor

(after *Solntse,* directed by Aleksandr Sokurov)

I.

I, Hirohito, among strewn boxes
and a fractured aquarium, compose
a poem based on a cherry blossom

and a dissected crab's revealed softness
as purebred goldfish on the lab's floor
strain for filtered water, "Sea in a Glass."

The Imperial lab floods with sunlight,
burning the eyes of rare porcupine fish
pried from their reefs for my further study.

Is it snow, or hot ash, progressing calmly
outside my blinded window, placing fire
on the flayed skin of this season's face?

I was a God in fancy human dress,
selected a fine top hat from London.
Forgetting my station, not minding where

I step, or what is stepped on beneath me
(a white, scuttling spider crab maybe)–
MacArthur floating on Tokyo Bay

I removed my divinity like a glove;
Petals away from a Chrysanthemum Throne.
The cold instruments of surrender signed–

a document to be skinned of whatever
fabric mere holiness is made up from,
I now stand before my smallest mirror

to observe ordinary nakedness.
Here is my entirely mortal hand
that may close upon a sea urchin's spines

to suffer the same pins and needles as
any human in the land. No longer
will trembling men button up linen shirts

or kneel in my bunker to explain how
a superior force borrowed the sun,
laying waste to our ancient paper towns.

2.

Today feels as much like winter as when
my father, Emperor before me, seeing
Northern Lights, impossible above Tokyo,

summoned me through four ministers
to speak of the sky's bright coruscations.
I have had to endure the long time

in which my wife and children lived
as if I were destroyed, under bombardment–
knowing their mourning as my own.

I missed the appointed afternoons,
when advisors would escort them to me,
so that I might present them long letters,

or read aloud from a masterful composition;
amateur of all, polyglot, ichthyologist,
I know the hours divided against us alleviate

our souls, make us speak new ways.
The sea forever inspires meditation
in peacemaker and noble warrior alike.

I measured my divinity in ocean-study,
so as to know, like common people who adore
the great ruler floating far above them,

each pulsing complexity under
the surface of alarmed, tentative waves
that always tremble like an organism

shocked or rattled by a sudden change.
I have looked at photographs of film stars also,
and felt great sadness for all living things

that move, to experience the minutiae of the day,
in a rock pool, which a greater eye envisions.
This much I learned from marine biology:

each way we mourn or find a motion
is determined by a higher instrumentality;
as if all creatures were forever in a bomber's sights.

Our bodies are examined by light's callipers, then
let drop, as if caught for momentary pleasure,
into the sea, which abandons, recalls, lifts and is.

Tokyo Elevator Girl

Ginza elevator girl, your sliding
white gloves operating doors in Wako

depto offer a flowing constraint, trained
to describe departments in gestures shy

yet free: the gifted stroke you impress
upon monotony makes any floating

creator envy your miniaturized
way: a slim balance, uniformed

perfection, a glide in control's
direction, art's stays. Your command of this

lifting cubicle with its set-piece play,
classically ruled to unfold in one time

and place, delights me. I'd rise with your levels
for hours, to honour this quiet

mastery, or descend to the ground floor
where the antique clocks are proudly displayed.

Hotel Oriental

sometimes the visible is the deeper world
Christmas lights in Shanghai

the rain is her leaving
a hotel is a room that you buy with minutes & days

the woman next door keeps your dollars in a tin box
a body is also a place you can wait in

gambling, until the end of longing
& thin walls let desire through

like rain-obscured radio or the click-click of vinyl
how you love is how photographs will remember you:

in dark suits, hair slicked back, slim moustache, a body
carrying itself like a film actor's

the rain projects its film on the green wall
& its ghost, its furrows

its slinking unfolding rivulets of time
every drop that falls has hurt you in its motion

each drop her heel in the hall, her
coming forward, going away

in the hotel you shared as each body shares its double
its mind, with some element of the visible

crossing through small square panes
of the opaque glass that sometimes appears to be

all there is of the present & surface, texture & reflection
how it stands behind us, this flat, deep screen

all that was good is a picture or a song
of her moving between lingering smoke & a dream

of a nightclub in Hong Kong where
nothing destined was wrong

if properly lit, red blue green
all that can be loved can be heard & seen

Northwest

Woke up in the house in *North By Northwest*
the one that flies out over the abyss.
What part of me is on microfilm?

When you were shot at the Grand Canyon
it was a fake bullet and fake blood
but you felt light as a glove in my arms.

It feels like disequilibrium to be walking here
amidst art from London, treachery from Russia.

Violent cultures produced my favourite authors.

Before the propeller plane comes to take me away
from the forest of small pines, the light shooting

through, may I admit that my body loves you.
My mind is quite another subject, as you suspect.
When I betrayed my nation I lost sleep.

Existence quickly becomes memorable, sadly.
In Vienna they taught me to ride horses,
speak with an American accent: *all aboard!*

I'm in Love with a German Film Star

Somewhere in Kansas or wherever Wichita is,
I stop to dally with a waitress in a summer dress

under a diner's neon kiss; I wear a UPS
uniform, drive for them. The name tag lies

when it says: G. W. Pabst. I make a highway
angel by slyly helicoptering sleeved arms

on the line that divides the independent cinema
of this scene. I have the ball cap and the smirk,

am filled with an unbearable urge to be always
thirty-two and to marry a girl named Miss Miss.

I'm filled with the luminous possibilities
of American landscape as it unfolds in movies.

If I was a plane I'd never have to land—
I'd be the land, you see, I'd already be the land

and the way wings spread over and below,
the way a shirt is also a stain is also a shadow.

Rainbow in Blackrock

You and I were pleased
to see both ends of it

grounded, somewhere far off
and to have the colours

so delineated, the arc bright
as yolk, as blood, as a fern.

We would have accepted
such a firm, full curve

spanning the bay's entirety
as our godsend for the week

so then, consider our pleasure
at this fainter one, sistering

its brighter other in the clever sky.
To see them both cupping the blue,

in sun and rain, was proof that sea
to land elide one light enjambment.

Modest Proposal

Every word counts, he said.
    And then he counted them.
        I saw my mother's dress.

It was in a garden and she brought
    Out a tossed salad, laid
        The plate on my lap as I read

William Carlos Williams;
    May; my body sixteen.
        How old was she? Thirty-seven

Or thereabouts. The tomatoes
    Were lovingly sliced.
        His look returned me to this.

If it is poetry, no need to ask,
    He added. Use your fingers
        As when you comb your hair

Before going in to see the one
    You will ask to marry, mirrored
        In the hall, the clock a heart

And the words throat-clotted,
    The tie poorly handled. There.
        How many words for the task?

Not the number, the distance.
    The sum of how to rightly say
        Hope under pressure's light.

It isn't what you write down
    That carries the full weight;
        It's what they heard, and why.

And so I went in and was shy
    And turned my phrases. She
        Told me to go to blazes.

I turned, when she held on and on.
    The altar vow has only so many words
        For how darkness binds, goes bright.

Mixed Tapes

There are whole mountain ranges,
highways in Croatia,
long broad sweeps of coast and sea,
that were listened through, years ago,

on mixed tapes that now lie boxed;
we listened, as the sun went by
and through and across
and into, your blonde hair,

both of us absorbed, it seemed
by the day and its travels.
Music's kiss lied.
It promised good eternal things,

not just experiences
that felt eternal as they passed;
now, sorting these tapes
marked religiously in green ink

I can recall none of the old songs,
though you still play:
beautifully, in that red top,
above the motor's hiss.

Brando

You weren't Stella, I wasn't Stanley.
We never had the heat or the bare bulb
coloured with a hood, didn't ever
quarrel nights over Napoleon's code,
law's cheap dividends. I never wore
a t-shirt, oiled in sweat, a Polack god
swaggering from sex, bourbon and pride.
You never made it up with me after,
your angel wings stuck back on with string.

We never aroused the neighbours
or lost ourselves breaking out of life
via love-making's bending of the bars;
we never got that escape from Sing-Sing.
I never boxed your sister into a corner
or tore her manners to tatters, a cat
adept with claws that catch the tin and slide.
We could elide the one thing and the other
but we never taught ourselves that play

or took that kind of New Orleans ride.
We couldn't outdo Brando, barely tried.
I once asked you to consider my ring.
You let me kiss you once or twice, hung up
the phone. Marlon, I hope, would've shown up
at your door, and let it be known he was
not to be denied, expressing madness in his method,
acting full-grown, wild. He'd have won you,
I'd wager. His strut, his form, his danger

and blown-out grace; he had an emperor's
face; was gross and beautiful in one
corpulent bet with a body's two-sided
coin. A genius, then, at being Janus.
Had he aimed for my teen dream-girl, would've
conquered her in drama class on day one
when we had to pair off, to read the parts
that broke us: I in my heart, you with other men.
I never shook off Kowalski's under-stain

pitting his shadow as he stalked, a panther
in a hot tenement cage; and you, Du Bois
or her sibling, doubled with rage, that such
a male was, at your stage, just so much raw
fiction. If only we'd been more brutal
to our fantasies, less controlled in
our diction, we might have howled out sex
to each other across the long dark summer
spaces, become passion's moving stars.

Gunn

moved between worlds, a motion
    in the very style took on;
        reformed the common, into something rare.

Jacketed muscle and passion for a uniform,
    revved engines, made language a throttle
        that roared with poise and sex and remorse.

Tossed love and its deadliness out
    as the first ball of the game;
        in and out of season, wrote of control, freely,

like a stone that takes, as it rolls, moss
    and other earthly bric-a-brac with it, to compose
        a song in the movement of its going; talent calm,

loins ruffled, Fulke Greville like a sock in the jeans;
    tested the means, renamed the terms of renewal.
        Became a sort of rocket fuel

for poems that, changed, from sea to sea, from Atlantic
    to Pacific, shone with American grandeur, retained
        some propriety: hard to do when boss

of desire's realm; when speeding down lines
    wearing flesh's delicate helmet
        for protection. Fallen, as all captains are, last-reel

come up on the high screen, at the drive-in where
    the Wild Ones would have been,
        acting out, tough—like any lover in a battle

knows that survival is a craft
    as well as a testing art; to keep the spear and arrow
    off the ever-beaten, ever-won heart.

Adult Return

How a man is visible
at Ingatestone, as the blue

and the night sky meet.
The reflection in the train:

concise haircut, suit.
Follow the unconcealed eye–

his face, a tree, a wire,
confront, refer, disengage, fly.

Woman at a Station

I see you off, as a woman at a station
her soldier, to the wars, unafraid of battalions
that smoke and whistle from windows as she

holds and holds, before releasing all his body,
his skin, scent, flesh, defined in the uniform;
the train goes, bearing away the adorations of

what was their joined ecstasy, unmarried love,
its little strategies of gin, fags, lamp-lit roses,
hugs and laughter in the park, the rained on rows

to which one returns, not alone with memory;
how the damp bed bears the impress of longing,
how long fingers know the mysteries of absence,

how the body lingers upon its own part in this.
To be a monk is not more or less than such as her;
the cramped travails are the same, the slow dust

gathering a dress of daily orders, flinging it on
one's shoulders in a sort of gay ritual, renouncing
hurt, or what hurt forgets to be, in all the flirting

and folly of the painted evenings, full of colour
and sad substance, the little that represents the all;
his lips and his heat are never against her, but on

her side; she reads the printed bulletins, knows
each manoeuvre as if the application of mascara
on to her own face; sees him fighting in a mirror;

is present in her mind on the field of confusion,
the battle is carried in her carriage, her motion.
So it is I see you off (my God) but cannot abandon

(even as I seek the immaterial spaces without sin
or longing) desire for you, for your attacked,
attacking body. How I aim to forget the cross

in favour of bled-out meditation, fragrant loss.
I hope you shall not return to take me up again
in your pinned arms, whirling me on a platform.

The Expedition

On the third day out we realized
we'd left half the supplies back at base.
The ice held our mood in check.
The radio transmitter was glazed

like a pea in aspic,
could no longer ping
our Morse or morose
SOS past the outer rim of things.

Day six the dogs died; Cedric "neglected"
to put out feed for them.
We ate the huskies, threw their bones aside.
Day seven polar bears, attracted by the remains,

began to stalk us. Day eight: *Cedric mauled.*
The rest of the camp sat appalled, gnawing
maps, the catgut from snowshoes.
Day nine, blizzards and no water.

On day ten, we reached the snow-blind pole.
Leopold, fingers half-blue,
showed me the rimed photo
of his wife and daughters. Day thirteen:

tent blown off by gale force winds.
Day fifteen: *Leopold dead.*
Sixteenth day. There's me, myself and I:
the rest not quite so fortunate.

Confessions

Language exceeds light & meat
and other doubtful propositions

that shape neither nature or truth, but
decorate teeth like dazzling gems.

My Universities

Debating the relative merits of Orchestral Manoeuvres In The Dark,
Or Tears For Fears, while April ice melts slowly in Westmount Park
Now appears to be less world-shaking than when, Misha G., we both
Could be smartly vehement about Richard Rorty, Boy George, Truth,
Logic & being spanked by Marianopolis twins known to us as Ruth.
Not that we were L. Cohen's heirs, but rather a pair of young pioneers
Gazing into the Future with our smoking jackets for uniforms, sayers
Of sooth but more often faux-decadent imbibers of lascivious perfumes,
Who often drank tea (before it was Pennyroyal) on mornings as Winter
Dripped away as surely as Youth does–as children crushed on looms;
If such industrial imagery seems a tad stark, consider the Reagan Years
Were also ours in Montreal; we danced: slim Japanese New Wavers,
The Cure & The Smiths, if not allies, our aural neighbours; felt Time's
Axis turn as early Eloquence (our praxis) dried up in Age's Summer.

Natural Curve

I watched a tree all day, it did not move.
This suggests to me a kind of love.
Nature is what you say it is.
Say it is Heaven or Hell.
What you choose.
In this dwell.
God proves.
See her.
Go to.
Ah.
O.

Communal Garden

May takes hold of summer's handlebars and wobbles on.

II.

Can it be that I still actually exist?
My body is so shrunk that there is hardly
anything of me left but my voice....

Heine

The Call

The call, when it came
Was Hong Kong quality:
Could have been from
The next room; which it was.
I wasn't glad to take it
But the phone rang and rang
And in reverse. The voice
Kept saying *cockles-mussels*.
I went and took the call
And now and now
We're gathered here, that is all.

Radio

Radio came at all hours, on different days.
Sometimes they were my father, dressed down
for baseball, on his bed, and all was good;
then there was "Father Robert Johnson," crazed
with The Lord, whose call-in shows were doomy
with late-night suicides and talk of Sodom's sins;
then, the house dark, that man's gilded voice
spent its charity on emptiness; my father snored.
I lay awake until the morning news, and dawn,
amazed that the end was upon us, none spared
except the ones who took Him into their souls,
then got up to sassy jingles for designer jeans
and snowstorms, which some weeks God sent.

Onset

Everything's changed that once was the same:
the sun that kept its golden hair combed

has grown dirty locks; the long sunlit sky,
blue as the sea, has turned off-milk like an eye

broken in battle. The clouds bruised by
winter storms are grey. The wild birds,

lofty as gods, have taken flight from us.
The wind, once leonine, has fattened

on its legend, and lies around. The stream
which used to rustle like Sylvan leaves

now slouches with mud in its mouth, far
from its youth and eloquence. How I wish

I had been born in a time before time, when
none of these natural, beautiful things

could be taken from me. All is memory
that once was rushing full aflame.

The Last Blizzard

My mother showed me
the house she'd lived in
fifty years ago

when she was a girl
who threw glass
at her enemies

with a pig named Margaret.
My father kept his eyes
on the deteriorating conditions

ahead, saying: *soon we won't see*
a thing in front of us.
For now, we could.

The town my mother
no longer lived in
had big wood homes

with long, wide porches.
Fir trees stood nearby.
Christmas lights. At the end

of her street the river was met
by a green bridge.
As we crossed we saw icy water.

My mother pointed out
a view that had once been
on our two-dollar bill, before

counterfeiters forced them
to use a more intricate design.
She showed me her school,

where she had walked and run,
then where she moved to later on.
So what if the weather made us slow?

We stopped to watch
a white deer standing
in a white field, not moving.

The Trees of Saint-Lambert

are having a field day
in the minds of my mother
and father, who live there

and open their window
to autumn, like a camera
working in light's favour.

Mother, Father, please come over.
No, stay. I will come to you.
No harm done, no harm. Father,

I forgive, give me your arm. Mother,
I know and understand.
Your other hand.

I Go to a Game with My Vigorous Father

I carry my father in hospital sleep,
Wake to light that devours things,
Each night a new drowning.

New summer air recalls old summers
When hand-in-hand, younger,
The live baseball stadium was there,

With its Expos players, and mustard.
Delected air, that food, now seem
As good as if pure Jesus came again.

Oh, that He would visit here to cure
Cankered layers that make bread out
Of any modest body. A body

Cannot keep up with all the jilt-jolt pace:
Science, that trying, changes in us–
Won't often be weighed down by

Too much mid-July-wheeling faith.
I feel levelling opaque bodies fold
One on one, as I have grown a son

From my father's negative-active cells;
And take that rapid son of his from
My smashed-open head–and hells

Gush down like Niagara, Victoria
And all geographic falls–
Those rich, long places. Vindictive nouns

Cultivate far inside my lovely Tom
Like fast bees that build white honey
From their nameless industry.

Comb my father's white hair
Where it was not aggressively shaved
For the scarring. But a game is saved

For his pitted memory. He sees
A white-dirted ball fly in blue air, a boy,
His own it may be, moving by his tall side.

Winter Work in April

I become winter and winter's man
to serve winter in its slow work;
my beard grows like the long span
of some white bird's wing. A stork
is a bird, just as winter is a season.

Having put on winter and winter's cloak
I stalk the white halls, a full blazon
of snow aloft in my long hand
like a new torch. I fold out to expand,
as winter's clock ticks on and on.

"Local Girl Dies of Frostbite"

I am cold and tired and must lie down
in my white nurse's dress,
five hundred paces from my town,
the air in snow-distress.

A storm which made me bed the ground
I never kissed; the warmth
that now escapes my body whole
will not be missed, though found

am a princess felled by a blackthorn—
a simple cold spell—
close to houses where I was born.
If you could rub my blood to burn

all would be grateful, so not to mourn.
As it is, I wear a virgin's winter crown.

Riverside Drive

Take that good road, driver
along the St. Lawrence

river. Spring sails ice
as boats sail now.

Take your time,
I want to see the houses

built centuries ago,
by the Seigneurs.

Turn here.
We're almost home.

I can smell winter.
I see the old porch ahead.

This is the avenue where
I loved and read.

Thank you for coming this
way, my favourite

route—a little longer,
but I enjoy the view

across the water,
the skyline. Where

do I live?
This address, in my head.

The Surgery

The mall of the night sends out its crossing lines,
Its vast dark piazza where children sleep away
All the playful things of their day; this is opaque,
And has the silence of silence in its muted block.
Lie here on the private square and feel public dark
As the lights invade the ceiling, cast from the park;
Or the cold beam that sweeps in, across the lanes
That divide the chasms from the surgery, whose
Windows, high as storks, with cross-hatching
Panes, emanate a piercing yellow light that pins
The thought of immortality onto the wall above
Where a head looks up into mortal reverie, to find
Those peripheries of blank colour define the canvas
On which the paint of desire dries each phantasm.

Comedian C.

Know this now: I long ago gave up my belief in Rapture.
I rise on pins and spit the pips.
Prenuptials must not include
Recourse to jelly donuts.
Not this time.
I too despise, abhor, deny, and denigrate prose poetry.
Drive me like a Porsche.
I am in. In luck. Intemperate.
Somebody better call the cops, kiddo.
Egghead marries hourglass.
Four-eyes weds egg-timer.
Old-timer shacks up with dish.
Creep gets world famous chick.
Tut Tut! Said McGinty. He said this with much relish.

The Wedding Photographer

It is a private, lonely thing
To do, gathering new pictures
Of delight. I take photographs

That build their album, the looking
Backwards, developing beauty:
Their standing, happy, just married

After the light has altered them.
No one sees me on my own bed
Later, rehearsing a vision

In which a white dress lifts then falls
With the sequencing of seasons,
Just and ordered in what happens

To bodies that love, are desired,
As fire, that takes a forest down
As dogs will a stag, cannot know

The king inlaid, uncovering
Vows future-arrowed, as cut skin
Shows the purple all wear within.

I Empty My Wallet

Movie we saw *(Frida)*; lottery ticket that didn't win
(01 02 06 09 30 31) bought a week after we married.
Receipt for a coffee shop in Hungary I used to name
Café Alibi. "Your final fitting is"–a stub for my
Wedding suit. I'll keep that. From Istanbul, costing
4.000.000 TL. With the blue mosque on it, number
648817: is it whimsical to wonder who was 648819?
You were 648818, of course. Le Nemrod, our place
In Paris. Lundi 15 Septembre we paid 37,70, total.

I see 1 CRÈME BRÛLÉE; 1 ASS FROMAGES;
1 FILET DE HADDOCK; 1 SAUC ROTTE
TRUFFADE. Was there wine that evening?
One forgets one's own habits, such clutter
Redeems the time's trivial paraphernalia, partially.
What else? Now what started as a chore, a duty,
Almost becomes an excavation: but I won't go
So far as to claim it forms the basis of an art.
It's still work though, to go through the forms,

The tattered bits of paper, one thinks to tuck away,
As if to be reclaimed, a proxy for a moment
That seems propitious enough to deserve a memory,
But too brief or petty to be guaranteed one, untokened.
ENTRÉE À GRANDS APPARTEMENTS
GALERIES DES GLACES. Yes, I recall a quarrel
Here, amidst much glass and circumstance.
SALLE 1 GAUMONT MONTPARNASSE.
A film but this time no title. We saw it 22/11/02.

A counterfoil for Twenty Pounds, stamped
111 BAKER ST LONDON W1 17. FE 04.
All these dates, and no exams to test them.
Here's one for shoes. A CARTE DE FIDÉLITÉ.
We won't be using this again. Nine squares
Will stay unstamped with the blue smudge.
We weren't faithful, in our fashion, to these people.
I go deeper, looking for something with resonance.
Your dentist: Nadia. No. The ticket to Bath,

From where I returned, after the crash. No.
Then this: a scrap, a note that looks full of ideas:
Colin Wilson?; Ben Hecht?; Doc Strange?;
Bermuda Triangle; and the number, *52.*
Is this the core of the novel I never wrote?
Some fascination with a chain of personages,
Places, that came to promise good creation?
Finally, a small silver thing from Knock: PRAY
FOR US. Someone should, at every little station.

Regent's Park

"a rustle / Of leaves in Regent's Park"
Louis MacNeice, *Autumn Journal*

You had asked me to bruise
the rosemary with the pestle
in the small white mortar
we had bought together
only a week before.

I wrestle with the loss
of you. It stands out, in Regent's
Park, by the gated drive,
in a London Fog coat,
like the security guard

on his phone in the rain,
as we passed the other night,
the branches above us all
about to break and fall
in the gale. Earlier, they had

come down in Leicester,
and three people died
from trees. Logic suggests
most will keep their vaulted
ceiling and not go to ground.

Maida Vale

After, how the after flows, as she runs out the door,
Runs to the circled park and undergoes lights there,
Dark as the New Year was, and house-provoking, too,
Wind the radio warned would come, and, untrue,

Broke a promise to let the day go on as still as brass,
Brass no hand has worn down or moved, at last;
How few things stay as promised, though many do—
Let us be thankful for the flowing of those, before,

Things in places that have never run off, rain-inked,
To go and change their names like marriages might;
Breakfast was her time to lie in bed and be high king;
It was the rain that sounded like woodwinds tuning,

Was it not, or the grass by the shore that appeared
Untimely, as Lear was, at his loose end, poor thing;
All wind is good-new as it flows on over the lip of fair
And foul, on-shaping the world like a caress does hair;

She was running, and after, returned to shower, when
On the radio MacNeice was saying *roses* and *snow*
Then, looking, our own garden was in the night, aglow.
After, how the after begins, as she tossed her gold hair.

The Mountain Lion

(i.m. Ian Hume)

We thought of winter
     when we saw the lion.
          Down from the mountains,
    no prey,
he made the impossible sudden

in snowfall.
    As close as, say,
        that tree.
    Still, very much a part
of each instant going.

While defining speed
    for us, our hearts, slowing,
        became the ice
    we'd raced on.
Such is vision's mystery.

It puts beauty deep
    into winter's chill.
        Fast as breath saying itself,
    he was gone:
a lithe accident,

meaty flood, rusted-gold;
    a fur-wreathed kingdom
        on the rangy slope;
    a mouth of stars
at earth-level.

The Recording Artist

"Wonderful, wonderful"
Johnny Mathis

My father, among other things, was sometimes sad
And he also sang, just like Johnny Mathis, to us
At night, seated on the left hand of our pillowed heads

His face turned slightly upwards, gracefully, to the side:
The image and sound of him I had when he died–
So that, despite the many hours when he cried out

This memory, not the others, will rise to mind–
Not in order to prove that love is better than suffering
But to record, in my deepest groove, his tenor's loveliness.

Action Comics

Tom Swift sold Action Comics
Outside the Amazing Gladstone's
Theatrical Acts of Illusion

To men and women in Forties hats
Who'd pay a nickel for diversion,
Some men stooping for *Blackhawk,*

Women reaching for *Plastic Man.*
Far beyond the magician's curtains,
A fighter pilot was sawn in half

By a Jap's ack-ack, or some German
With a sneer would make the heroine
Disappear with rope and a blackjack.

All this action without applause,
In the theatre of war, that long winter
Sometime just after '44, when

My mother was born, in Quebec,
Unaware my father would sneak
Up on ice skates and blind her eyes

With mittens like the fold
Gladstone tied round his assistant's
Pretty face, but not as cold.

A House That Was Perfect for Them

After they moved, they stayed.
It was said *it had been a house*
that was perfect for them.
So they could not leave.
As he lay dressed for burial
they kept on about that other house,
the one in the woods, up a fir-brushed lane:
in winter, held by snowfall, in summer
its wood sides brown as the sun-dark lawns
when the rain stayed off. Each of its rooms
clock-sung, the ticked chimes a music
to escort one room to the next,
as if the long bookshelves in them
wanted a clock's endless company.

The Man Who Killed Houdini

My father, when alive,
Loved to suck his stomach
In, and urge us
To ball a fist and strike
A blow, straight
To his solar plexus

Erect as Houdini should've
Been, but in the story
Never was. I'd put
My small hand softly
Against his strong flat
Gut, and push, afraid

To lay him low,
To kill him like the great
Houdini—so well did he
Describe the murder-jab
To me. And he'd fall down
Then rise in laughter.

III.

... winter winter tennis....

Samuel Beckett

Writing

Say what you will,
it can only tell
what you know.
The words, in order,
have to confess
how you starve
or bless
the beautiful.
The caution or
progress
must reveal
which parts
you'll trust,
which discard.

Envoi

Send out the loveless children,
those faceless ones, pansies,
droops, suckers and ragamuffin
losers, tooth-short, bedraggled,

gaggle geeks, off-strumpets
and low-levels, send them out!
Let them prowl devil-streets, selling
pock-skin, pencil shavings, eye-

lashes and TB-dolls. Fix them;
spike their drip-feed with Benzedrine.
Keep the comfort-zones clean.
Send these poppets, these tinsel-

Hansels and sappy-sonnets, these
Gretel-stanzas fetching nopes, into
the hands of craving-warts, stucco
borders, palsy-gangs and semi-dopes.

The nasty-edit dopamine cabal are
zoot-impaired, pleasure-pained, unused
to pretty things, flowers, a kind note.
Send my soul to the print-alley fiends.

Hydra

I did not know my own good breathing yet,
Waited on the land while you swam out far.
Rhythm cuts to feel the Hydra teething.
A heart's withholding ache is a line fear.
Voice trips the force after the stutter but
I halt to extend, to give, to utter
As a lover on the brink of water
Ponders the leaping pool where sunlight lies.
Sun's all surface where rocks break beneath
And many are the divers who have died
Joining their form with the forms below,
Hot to imply their safety was fluid–
Their falling lines a force to fly and flow.
Ceasing to be I sense my mind in blood.

The Mosquito and the Map

You dawdle on the cartography of conquest
In the tent where Caesar stabs his ring finger
On the Tiber. Dare you nibble the Emperor
As he repels a disappointing triumvirate?

Or have you already tried it, pre-emptively?
Is that why the God-King bleeds tidily,
Nit-picks his neck, looks wan at the future?
No. Daredevil blood-pilot now you dive.

The Shape of Things to Come

appears to be a trump of doom;
is like a hollow room; a horn
of plenty; a ballerina's

shoe; a house in Whoville,
a devil's mouse; a bang-drum,
a pirate drunk on deadman's rum;

like a broken broom used to brush
the webs from day-dreaming boys
in math exams; a rack of lamb;

a donut convention; a depleted
pension; the sort of position
churchmen don't like to mention;

is shaped like a poem mute and dumb;
like a big bronze bell held by
a handlebar-moustachioed

strongman working for Barnum;
like a sausage and French mustard;
seems to be hoist on its own petard.

Marcus Makepeace

Dr. Ezekiel Lightning's Players left their snail meniscus
Behind with cat-o-nine-marks upon Makepeace's loins.

A troupe of tall wrestling women dressed like Lincoln
The night he died: theatrical this; and Marta Monocle

Who was said to have sirloin-branded the devil: an S
Beef-sizzled on that red character's tan hide. Marcus

Hissed his pleas to Jesus to be freed from promises
Made in Madame SoSo's billowing tent, fiery-lit by

Wax made from the bees that had gorged on flowers
Growing by the very cross on which our Saviour died.

The honey-blood scent of those candles–Little Ava
Largent dealing cards–the chips made from narwhal

Tusk (some claimed unicorn)–while Dexter Oliphant
And his Amazing Ambidextrous Sinners deviated a bit

From the norm, guzzling gazelle mucus from a horn.
The very scene master Hieronymus had dreaded was

Now the fire-curtain on which our friend lay and wept,
As if twin juggling harpies from Norway had born him

A noseless son, who would cut and shuffle angel bones.
He bawled in his stovepipe mewing for fiends to revisit.

The Ministry of Emergency Situations

During an emergency, all
Wedding rings must be removed
And citizens will be asked to
Undress in the streets. The Ministry
Will bathe those affected with
Disinfectant Foam. They must ensure
Their eyes are shut. Those who refuse
To take off jewelry, tokens
Of affection, clothes, will be shot.

The fully naked will dance in
The medical shower, then be
X-rayed and scanned by magnets.
Inspections will go on. The cleansed
Will be allowed to request
Compensation for their torn rags,
Irradiated keepsakes.
The Ministry of Songs will form
A choir, and douse them in anthems.

The Oil and Gas University

The sectors interface. In Novosibirsk
She wears a hooded parka. She
Challenges outmoded ideas. She
Transforms the education-research

Manifold and provides new incentives.
She pulls her hood back to reveal
That beauty achieves real excellence
In a real-world setting. Her lips

Hit each of the seven key targets
Set by the national institute last year.
Ownership and exploitation
Have no place in this exciting dynamic.

Opportunity, however, is vital here
In this oil and gas region near the pole.
She walks past the infrastructure.
The gas flares in the fields, the tundra

Reciprocates under the white solar
Glare–then continuous darkness
Of course will eventually supplant this
Brilliant feat. High technology

Must provide a nexus and intensive
Inventories. She is beautiful and I
Wish to introduce myself to her
At the Oil and Gas University.

Sunflowers in Rostov

*"The Rostov Region is the largest
producer of sunflowers."*
Unesco

*"Rostov, the headquarters for Russia's
creaking Chechnya war machine."*
The Guardian

The Rostov Region is the largest producer
of sunflowers. For this reason alone, I must

go there, in summer, to see the yellow bounty,
to participate in this blinding harvest.

Please do not try to stop me.
My ticket is well and truly bought.

I leave tomorrow. To have
never been to Rostov, to have never seen

their sunflowers, must count as one of life's
richest, most notable, loss-sorrows.

The Firebrand

until it plays itself away
holds green in,
burning and being burnt

in one long hand–
one short hand–
always shorter

the eye in which it sees
the new fire
is its own

The Serious Business

The serious business is the world's too-much-with-us;
The warming surface and the freezing-beneath fuss;
Cross-slat sunlight dazzles the upturned model's bum
In some studio in Ravenna, or Paradise, a grand sum
Of *nada* incorporated. I have been five times a day
On the carpet, to defray my fear that God has fled

Not to be extradited. Let me state the fifty-year problem,
Excited: the shallow end of the pool is where beauty
Exfoliates but the deep is where one rises through various
States (how water flows like the lost bride of Milton)
Bent out of shape but oxygenated for final union
With blood of the lamprey (lamb's prey) adept at the slide,

Slip, slow-fast-slow thrum of ideation, that empty condom,
Verse creation. Julia's liquefied plastic, coiling the surge's
Pulse knows a lapse-soon into superannuated what-else.
Should we barricade the fights, or splurge our corpuscles
On the trident of this jangle folly, life's hustle-bustle?
I call for substance, *décorporation,* being not-useless.

Winter Winter Tennis

When a child, I was a reed.
People bend. Straw burns, too.
And burning mends. The air has faith
in smoke signals, having had them
in its ways. Sheaves are fruitful.

The person you're kindest to
is the one you want to save. Fire owns
the ruins it creates. Ash on the brow
means only one love inside the mind.
Thieves in the temples means a cold.

Want to grow old and take down
this book. Want you to know me
as someone who once had a look
and a place to call their town. Voted
for a mayor who kissed a rose.

There was also a pink child in the frame
and what's her name. He won, he won,
they over-proclaimed. Ran races
of boys through villages, trailing flames.
Am this, this way, this very same.

Wouldn't see it any other way.
Should this enter woodlands where
poplars recreate, overturn the maypoles,
suckle ancestral possibilities ho! of tone;
born alone hey! in a cloud of verbal turns.

Taking Tea with Charles Bernstein

Lapsang Souchong with a lapsed *sous* chef;
Charles enjoys its smoky aroma and tarry taste.
Keemun with a Communard;
Charles delights in a lightly-scented nutty flavour.
Yunnan with a U-turning UN man;
Charles likes the maltiness with milk.
Gunpowder with Guy Fawkes;
Charles notes the soft honey taste, the little bang of it.
Chun Mee with Connie Chung;
Charles raises his eyebrows at its smoothness.
Oolong with Long John Silver;
Charles eschews milk and sugar, not wanting them
    to dominate.
Ti Kwan Yin with a typist quite intuitive;
Charles swoons at the fragrant infusion.
Pouchong with Pol Pot;
Charles is suspicious of the very sweet, stylish taste.
Pai Mu Tan Imperial with a pretty tanned empress;
Charles notes the small buds of this rare, white tea.
Yin Zhen with L. Cohen;
Charles spits out the silvery needles.
Jasmine with a *Jass* band;
Charles sits in with Bix and finds delicate modern time.
Rose Congou with a Belgian from the Congo;
Charles admires the great skill used in the handling
    of the leaves.
Earl Grey with Duke Ellington;
Charles considers this mandarin blend a tad traditional.
Darjeeling with Jar Jar Binks;

Charles celebrates with the "Champagne of Teas."
Dimbula with Dmitri Shostakovich;
Charles sips the light, bright, crisp tea; his mouth feels fresh.
English Breakfast with Edie Sedgwick;
Charles likes this strong bed tea.
Afternoon Tea with Anthony Blunt;
Charles bites into a cucumber sandwich.
House Blend with Olivia Hussey;
Charles is comforted by the type most people use at home.
Bubble Tea with Bazooka Joe;
Charles is amused by this beverage with tapioca balls.
Iced Tea with Richard Blechynden;
Charles, hot by now, is refreshed by this ice cold drink.

Opium and the Romantic Imagination

Close the door when you go, sweetheart.
The opium of the breeze from
that day we danced in close comfort
feels strong. Begun, simply, went on
from there. Glimpses, hair. Strands amid
doing wrong. Time is a popular
song I won't remove from my mind.

London Property

Writing passes. In the street it tips its hat. Horses, bearing a closed set of events in a long box with a name for a body, clip. Stones react to passing feet like objects. Trade is poor during a downpour. After rain more is purchased. The men have purchase on all available books made by other men in august hats; they tip, hail and ride, with spurs and gloves; sometimes a companion. Writers bow, grateful to have stones touch their shoes. Rain gathers praise for sunnier times. A lady with an artificial hand stifles a mouth brought on by an evening that has dared to interrupt her novel with its forensic deliberate colours; the lurid air murders the day with little fingers born to play Chopin but tutored instead on macabre vices. *Langoustine!* Somewhere an idiot sailor clumsy with children is taking a boat outside to sink it deep. Suitors are leaping like deer in the park; a window dresser declines to hang a suit with the notorious sign of Madame LeBoeuf. *Woof! Woof!* A cop is detected inserting diction into tone. More on the beat, or lambs that bleat their identities will do; listen to the wind, it's planning to go and blow your horses down. Houses are lit all night to solidify the books immense and valid under bright well-managed locks. She throws her lips back really to implicate the sound of desire if made by a lion. He composes a lid upon a mournful crescent.

Some Clarity

The problem with problems
is the meaning of moaning:
Being and Boeing,
the cat and the whip,

the wrist and the rust, the action
in the Winchester, the Colt,
Ben Franklin's lightning bolt.
The pose is to smirk but cry,

jitter-bug but be frozen,
try to be immobile on Vodafone,
write white with bruise-ink,
a stick turning sick in the sink

doodling Gyro Gearloose alphabetics,
Unca Edison running the supply,
while all the birds at Bletchley Park
sing on their enigmatic Qwertys.

Bert and Ernie swap brown shirts
and the popular and the arcane
switch and prance. Language,
that strange badge of honour,

sips Bombay gin in some storm warning
as an embodied urge to sleep together
tucks into books: ratiocination
the only ball-gag in this one-ponygirl town.

Vocal Range

When will poets get over words? They moon
And gloat on them, as if owners of origins, are on
Top of the motion that moves the heavens or
Moans in watershed winter. I tire of tongue-wet
Celebrations of glottals, the click, clip and clop
Of sounds throbbed together like rubbed lamps,
Jostled coins–poems a pocketful of poses. Too,
There's been a lot of jocularity slash lightness lately–
Many mentions of popular figures, movies, and TV–
Getting overmuch of the world crammed into crawl
Spaces under the text, sometimes even on top of it–
How much hipness can any master muster, then use?
I was savvy before I saw those I love die and cease.
Now I leave my slip, suck, swoon outside for prose.

Warming

Each day, the glacier at the pole of my walk
To the store where I buy stamps and milk
Diminishes, threatening the few species

Living on the floes of my more and more mild
Heart—the white bears that stalk feelings
Especially, are finding less and less wild

So, land-tamed and ice chipped back, fall
Into tepid water nearly warm enough to drink;
This inner tundra of my self is fraught,

As all tundra and all selves are, with caught
Nature, since natures prowl and thrive best
When least talked of and more talked through,

As if the mesh between prisoner and love
Let tongues cross between the cold grate
Without piecemeal cutting of their red kiss.

Seismic or simply a breaking off of a chunk
Of berg, then, this shift in clime, from frigid
To temperate, from morning to much too late?

And what is the flag or thermometer planted
At the beef-pink core of my claimed identity
Doing to the radius around that place,

That may or may not still be me, like waves
That radar-blip out like tea stains from the cup
Onto the paper, browning space circularly?

Can one finger of ice—an icicle maybe—
Expose itself to the frost, and be mine,
While another, cut off, tossed to dogs, lost—

Endures another winter or summer, unnamed?
This wilderness-warming is like an earthquake
Tamed, stroked down so it sleeps, a white cat

Curled against the ground, nice and flat;
The sky is flake on flake on flake of snow,
Which is all I know of winter, need to know,

For hell is ice and heaven blue sky thinking
There are clouds above. I miss my own dead,
Despite the cooling zones inside that run to spring.

Hammer Attacks on Treasures of Venice

Atop the arcade column
of the Doge's Palace
a delicate carving calls

for obliteration. The Madonna
near the church of San Pietro
di Castello, struck

with a sledgehammer;
the marble hauled off.
See the attacker from his

perspective. What appears as
demotion of the good is simply
misunderstood restoration.

Consider his focus on the materials:
shining stone, plaster,
wood and paint.

Objects robbed of nature
by design's hand,
cracked and ruined again

as when first found,
re-attain beauty.
He may have altered an angel,

reduced a frieze, rent a tableau
and shattered a pedestal
to low ground:

our madman has also found
a source lost in the ruins
of theology and making.

He's set an inhuman standard
for what is worth collecting–
not fine but finely ground: sand.

Ars Poetica

Purposelessness is an art
That animals
Have never mastered–
Haven't had to–
A line that holds its form
Hard to the sheet. Spin
Away, then, to some
Light in Argentina
A woman at the quay
A man in Panama
Darkness on the bay;
Seneca, writing a letter
To a young friend
On the best way to die.

Notes and Acknowledgements

Thanks to the editors of each of the following, where many of these poems first appeared: *Acumen; Agenda; The Alsop Review (Octavo); Babylon Burning; Chapman; Cimarron Review; Connaissances; Cordite Poetry Review; The Cúirt Annual 2005; Drunken Boat; Fortnight; Future Welcome; The Guardian; Jacket; Limelight; London Magazine; The Los Angeles Review; Magma; The Manhattan Review; Matrix; Natural Curve; New American Writing; The Oil and Gas University; Other Magazine; Otherwheres; Pages; Paper Tiger; Radio Waves; Sandstone; Seam; Square Lake; UEA MA Poets Anthology; Upstairs At Duroc; Vallum; west47 online,* and *The Wolf.* Many appear here in somewhat revised form.

I would like to thank Denise Riley and George Szirtes for their work with me on more than half of these poems, during my study at UEA; as well as my classmates from the UEA MA course, especially Karen Wortley, Nathan Hamilton, and Jenna Butler.

The following poets read some or most of these poems and offered invaluable suggestions over the period of this collection's coming together: Siobhan Campbell, Patrick Chapman, Alfred Corn, Kevin Higgins, Lachlan Mackinnon, Alex McRae, David McGimpsey, Eric Ormsby, Sally Read, Carmine Starnino, Andrew Steinmetz, Rachel Warrington, David Wevill, and John Hartley Williams. I wish to thank them here for their generous advice.

Robert Allen (1946-2006), poet, writer, editor, teacher, friend, was an inspiration for many years. His death in 2006 was a great loss. Jason Camlot is always my ideal close reader and his attention to these "language acts" is most appreciated. Special thanks to Steve Luxton, who wrestled the poems here to the ground and demanded that most at least made sense.

My beloved wife Sara Egan is my truest guide.

Close friends have also shaped my thought during the period when this book was written especially Thor Bishopric, Peter Forrest, Fr. Oliver Brennan and Dr. Sass. Much love to my mother and brother.

My father, who was diagnosed with brain cancer in March 2005, died September 9, 2006, in Montreal, where he was born. His presence and absence marks this collection in terms of its key themes of wit, love *and* bereavement.

Todd Swift was born in Montreal and grew up in St-Lambert. He served on two occasions as The League of Canadian Poets' representative for Quebec. His poetry series *Vox Hunt* (1995-97) was hailed by *The Globe and Mail* as "virtually unique in North America." From 1998-2000, he was the Visiting Lecturer at Eötvös Loránd University, Budapest, specializing in courses on poetry and film. In 2001, he moved to Paris, then to London, England, where he earned an MA in Creative Writing from The University of East Anglia. His poems have appeared in journals such as *Poetry Review, The Guardian,* and *New American Writing,* as well as on ABC, BBC, CBC, and RTE radio. He is poetry editor of Nthposition.com and edited *100 Poets Against the War* (Salt, 2003). He has reviewed for *Books in Canada, Poetry London* and *The Dubliner,* among others and has been Oxfam Great Britain's Poet In Residence since 2004. His latest publication is a collection of essays entitled *Language Acts* (Vehicule, 2007), the first major study of Anglo-Quebec poetry in over 40 years, co-edited with Jason Camlot. Swift lives in London, England, with his wife Sara.